Layers of Un

Also by Mark Goodwin

Else
Back of A Vast
Shod

The Shearsman Chapbook Series, 2012

Seren Adams : *Small History*
Kit Fryatt : *Rain Down Can*
Mark Goodwin : *Layers of Un*
Alan Wall : *Raven*
Michael Zand : *The Wire & other poems*

hors de série
Shira Dentz : *Leaf Weather*

Layers of Un

Mark Goodwin

Shearsman Books

First published in the United Kingdom in 2012 by
Shearsman Books, 50 Westons Hill Drive, Emersons Green
BRISTOL BS16 7DF

Shearsman Books Ltd Registered Office
30–31 St. James Place, Mangotsfield, Bristol BS16 9JB (this address not for correspondence)

www.shearsman.com

ISBN 978-1-84861-248-8

Acknowledgements

Some of the poems selected for this collection have been published or
accepted for publication by the magazines *Shadowtrain* and *Shearsman*.
Thank you to the editors.

'Sun-Fall & Tools' was written as part of my Writing East Midlands
'Write Here' Leicestershire Landscape Poetry Residency, 2011. My thanks
to Catherine Rogers and the WEM team. 'Gar Den O' Membrance' was
written as part of my Loughborough University Poetics of a Campus
Residency, 2012. Thank you to the Loughborough University Development
Trust for funding. And thanks to Leah Graham and Kerry Featherstone for
support and collaboration on this project. Acknowledgement must also go
to the following inspiring creative writing students: Chris Bates, Samuel
Hardy, Sophie Hyde, Samuel Lane, Natalie Moores, Tosha Taylor.

Thank you to Ady Adams for critical and vital creative contribution during
the making of 'Wrecked Balance in Castle Zawn', all those years ago!

Thanks to Brian Lewis for the 'seed' line: 'partially eradicated staircase'.

I am lucky enough to have a meticulous proof-reader who knows my
work very well. Thank you to Julia Thornley for vital critical and creative
contribution, and also for rigorously testing every last tiny but apparent
inconsistency in this collection.

Thank you to Tony Frazer, for the usual easy-yet-careful Shearsman
way of collaborating.

Much amazed gratitude to my partner Nikki Clayton, as ever, for
faithfully and encouragingly accompanying me on various kinds of
journeys, and also for her splendid photo of Casteal Tioram, which is the
first layer of 'un' on this chapbook.

Contents

For Ady

Sun-Fall & Tools, a Watermead Park, a Charnwood, a May 2011

the live man climbed
onto the top of a turf-roofed
birdhide

the birdhide's iron door was padlocked
the man sat on the roof's long-grass mattress

with its breeze-block walls
and camou'd over roof
the birdhide reminded
the man of an ordnance pillbox

he was tired
tired of many of his life's parts

for a while he stared at the swirls
& flow of duckweed & scum close
to the old gravel pit's shore

the sky held cathedral-grand clouds
spring sun lit floating seed-fluffs
& the up-down dance of gnats

a duck & her so-far-five
-surviving 'lings scottled across
the lake's sparkling membrane

swifts & martins let loose stripes of screech

he observed closely the flow of bits
across the lake's surface
the vortex curls & accelerations

then he lay down on the birdhide's turf roof
closed his eyes and instantly
the sun fell into his face like

a sudden home finding an ancient building

after another while

a while of faint red pulsations
& black fang-wing shapes
on his eyelids' insides

he gently turned his face away
from the nuclear-fusion explosion
so as not to blind himself

and he opened his eyes

small fast black alphabetic aeronauts
swifts & martins
were being utterly all they could ever be
sliding through sky above him

they were totally unaware of any alphabet
and he knew nothing of the feel
of the smack of gnats gathering
satisfyingly in the back of one's throat towards
the end of a perfectly judged swoop

(you don't either and nor do I)

then with no warning
and with no decision
the man with his eyes wide open turned
his face back towards the star

that gushes photons over Earth

no reflex action came
his eyes remained staring
into the sun for many seconds
until an orangey inkiness

heralded something unknown
with flapping banners of shredded retinas

the man could clearly hear the air
& its flyers & the lake's ripples
& the waterbirds' motions
he could feel soft hummocky turf
under him and he could smell
the soft musk of grasses at once
fresh & ancient

but he could not believe

that he was now blind
he could not believe that his body
had failed

to slide protective skin over its eyes

o

walk down to the birdhide
at the side of the old gravel pit
see the steel door painted green

kept shut

for years with a shiny padlock

notice the tufts of grass that roof the hide

but what you will not see now
is the dead man's body decomposing
on the roof

the cadaver is beyond your line of sight
the site of the deadness is secret

although already there is sweet rankness
humming fetid on the spring air

o

       laid out in the sun
       on the turf on a roof
       of a locked-up birdhide
       beside an old gravel-pit

where perhaps once
the bones of a mammoth were found

I heard hard very solid boys approach

there was the ratchet of a
bike's back-wheel-spro
-cket & the wet
haaarrk tpuuuhh

of a lad gobbing

they were below me and couldn't see
I was there listening

to the gravel & silk
of their young masculine
Leicestershire accents

these were liminal-lads
off an estate on Leicester's
northern rim

I heard one say why
the birdhide I hid on top of was

    locked

    but as is
    the way with

    memory

    I can only say
    that I think

    the birdhide was once
    the site of a fire

    that by byelaws
    should not have been

    lit

o

blind & dead & badly mutilated
by the actions of bacteria
& jackdaws' beaks

with ligaments already detached from vital
musculature & bone connections

and with a veil of complex stink dressing him

a man climbs down off a birdhide's turfed roof
at a side of an old water-filled gravel-pit

first he finds a rail fence
and he balances along this as
precisely as a heron's stare

now he walks along a path through woods

running away through fresh spring growth
perpendicular to his path is an obvious trod
where kids have made inroads into

un-adult territories

he follows a trod in amongst trees crosses
a rail fence and now faces

an earth bank

an earth bank shows bare soil where feet
have scrubbed up its gradient

as he surmounts a bank's brow despite
his burned out eyes he's aware

      of a sofa in a clearing

he's aware
of a tangle of blue polyprop rope

& a fresh fireplace with kindling stacked neatly
with ripped-&-screwed-up newspaper

he smells two old pop-bottles sun-faded
one a quarter full of green sludge

as he descends
into some camp he is able
to notice

a wheelbarrow half-drowned at a gravel-pit's rim

on closer inspection he also becomes aware that
there are two good bow-saws with clean blades
their saw-tooth-serration is silvery & precise

among a green frilliness of nettles

he experiences further and notices a hammer
& a shiny almost brandnew adjustable spanner

now sitting on a glade's sofa
are two transparent children

they do not notice

his terrible stinking solidity
they are arm in arm talking

one's a boy one's a girl

there is a dead cat just
as inquisitive as our dead man

one see-through kid

for a moment sees this smudged cat
slinking but says nothing
of it and will say

nothing of it for all her long life

a dead man now clove-hitches
a hammer to a polyprop rope
and tightens a line between

an ash & a willow

a hammer hangs
as if being banged
down on a nail

by an invisible hand but
obviously held

in this position by a blue clove-hitch

where a rope is attached to an ash
it is twisted back on itself
for a metre or so along its length
making a double-thickness like
an extra hawser-lay

now our dead man inserts
a gleaming adjustable
spanner into these twists
so a spanner too is

suspended on a line

What A Dead Man Does
(un dated)

up a partially
eroded staircase past

one wall
gone where

wind & rain
have streaked

plaster with diagrams
of utter

nowhere known along

a corridor full
of smashed

-glass footsteps & drifts
of pigeon shit through

a doorway whose
frame is partly

in and
    partly out

of the doorless

hole it once
kept oblong

in a corner where
floorboards darken

under juices among

a pile of rags a
dead man does

nothing

     o

     yet

     o

his stench
thickens

to a solidity to a

shape that stands
a figure of gas

now walks its
remaining

memorable smells now

now walks its
form through

a doorless hole
and descends

a partly eradicated
stairwell to

a plain of waste
land droning

with a fizz
of worlds'

dissolving

each step this
shape of

stink takes

plants a new place
footsized on

ground forgotten
by no-one but

never remembered this

sickly fragrance now
now follows an old

urge along
a rim where

open fields meet
an excrescence

called *city* he

our gone-shape
pious as a

living Druid whipped
by leather words but

dead as an oak

     o

       door

     o

nail

he follows along all
along land on

an edge and
he pays none

of his attention

to walls or
any cordons built

by alive ones
who try to

keep each

place parcelled he
passes through

his gaseous
solidity slides

a faint vibration as
his form rubs

kerbs & rails &
walls but no

shape made
or imagined stops

his urge

to follow
follow all

     o

    all

     o

along an edge

Wrecked Balance in Castle Zawn, West Penwith an August a 2005

it's all moon's doing

moon amongst smokes
like a wrecked spacecraft

moon balancing a self

amongst clouds like-surf
-like-frail-fabrics and also

moon balancing sea's

tattered surf-rags
or swell-clothes

on & off edges
of land-flesh

it's moon's doing
moon strikes

a balance between

o

The moon undresses coast;
her gravity orchestrates striptease:

salt cloths, deep chiffons
& froths tugged off.

When tide's thick slippery veil
is all pulled back,

here part of a ship's carcase
is fully revealed.

The tease has exposed
bent & rust-red metal dead

still on the zawn's bed.

                    o

The wreck of the RMS Mülheim,

just a ship's stern, lies still
but like a building falling.

The wreck tilts
so its deck's a cliff. Fixed

amongst distance, behind
the drunk hulk, sky hinges on sea

—this horizon is crossed
where Longships Lighthouse rises straight up.

                    o

some god's vast child
dropped a toy and it exploded

fragments of wreck
are spread around the zawn

thirty-tonne slabs of iron like
chocolate melted bent by sunshine

the sea's white hands mangled
inches-thick steel as if it were liquorice

the huge white super-surf-hands ripped
at the hull and curled girders

it all looks like just after cartoon-action

but touch the cold dense metal
and adults-only clangs like a cracked bell

       o

the hull is pierced
by a granite shark's head

it is hard to fathom just
how hard that shark's head struck

the hull's skin curls out
from round the lips of its gash

seawater drips
from the dark hole

dangling cables
protrude & sway

parts of the ship's carcase
are now upholstered green with weed

pipes & girders are twisted
and jammed between boulders

an engine block & gears
have barnacles bolted to them

you balance
on a thick sheet of gritty-red steel

suddenly the high-pitch scrape-screech
the rusted metal emits as it flexes

against granite that mangled it
threatens to shatter your teeth

    o

the wreck is a ruined fort
smashed after the sea's seege

yet the sea still attacks
the silent & collapsed battlements

wave after wave of offensive salt
white hooves white knights white swords white lances

so slowly the fort erodes
its red rust perpetually weeping away

but the sea will not cease
until the last ghost is dissolved

    o

huge smoothed granite eggs
surround the wreck

my healthy balance allows
me to pick out
a code of stones to step along

with my agile locomotion I
tip-toe over
slippery algae-coated globes

with my feet & inner-ears
I easily read ground

    o

i step
from the zawn's bed
onto the wreck

climb aboard carrying

no baggage but hopes
for a still voyage
through a still ship

on a dry shore
suddenly sky's &
sea's blue hori

zon bends
through my head an
outside world slow

ly spins a
round an in
side of my skull i

've stepped into or
through a
fish-eye-lens

-world all swirls
the wreck
is dead

still jammed
fast on
granite but

all swirls
i'm a
bandoned

by surf
faces
where I can play

s my feet flat
offset lad
ders & st

aircases per
vert my cli
mbing all

a sick fun
-house skewed
kilter off whiff all

at sea yet really
just still no
role or yaw yet

my storm
ache stom
ach turns

turns into a
zawn cunt
aining

an iron chunk
being turned o
ver & jounced sc

raped bou
nced & sma
shed ag

ainst gran
ite gut
walls siz

zling salt
i stagger
with the

flung & un
balanced
weight of

soaked cargo

o

all aboard between
all corners & stairs
all house-shapes scream

all where & all else

all captains are memories
all dressed in silver buttons
all seamen are lost feelings

some faces are not bent railings
nor shapes scraped in paintwork

all aboard between
all between all
shores & all voyages

all on tip-toes or
all tongue-tips
all balanced boulders seem
all all aboard between

all froth white as whites of
all terrified eyes as
all balance collides

all else

all in all
all wrecks cross
all loss

Strontium & Gold, A December 2011

Strontian River's th
ick white cords wrig

gle & loop be
tween a glen's

he   athery wings
hill-f   og caps a

holl   ow-of-world
inno   cent of alchemy

now as if win   d had
torn a tr   ee-part

free & fl   ung
it through cl   oud a

dark broad bar soars

finger feath   ers gr   aze
wet air's vo

iceless noises some

lead-grey crea
ture-shape a

bout to be
gone pulls

gold to ground now

ea   gle claws fall
as cryst

all   isation
from sky's mine beak

punc   tures pelt sud
denly as if woun

ded   a loll
oping fea   thery

rock jerks
blood's bits

through grasses as

ele   ments repeat
edly f   lock &

scat

Note: *Strontian* is a river & a village in western Lochaber. In the 18th Century the hills to the north of the village were mined for lead. The element *strontium* was first isolated from the mineral *strontianite*, which was discovered in the mines.

Gar Den O' Membrance
a Luff Uni Campus,
a January a 2012

an I steps be
yond layer 1

through a 3
D printed

crypt
ogram

of iron gar
den gate

feet are autumn
oak leaves flat

orange brown
ground feelers

(feelers of
ground an

I is up

on) grass clinks sil
very spheres of

rain magne
tised by hopes

enfolded in
map-layer 2

here

is bent into
shapes of there

then (t)here is
printed as when's

roots

t(h)ree close
oak t(h)rees

point pins
@ a ref

erence gridding
an I's mind

6 metres to a my's left]
of nostalgia's scent
climb
saws rises
into a present
tense taste
of oa(b)ide

freshly sawn
pine scent

creeps its
creases across

smooth skin
s of things an

I's eyes take
from in

nocence &
map's layer 3

waits as A
black rect

angular hole
dug at The

back of a red
cottage hemmed

in by in

dustry's sylla
bles an I rem

embers forge

tting an I re
members for

getting dire
ctions as an

I remembers
forgetting

directions as
ground B(e)

comes A last
thought of

(b)ones
of *mine*

A Casteal Tioram, A Moidart,
A December 2011

a we fade
in tuned by a time's pin

point we flickers of selves clad
in Gore-tex as
hail sizzles our figures a we imagine
men in wool drenched &
ferocious congealed in centuries

isthmus sand plants

> an us as
> fresh foot
> steps as

ragged battlements hang
on a gabbro uvula in a Loch
Moidart's mouth we cross

> a thread of land we

approach a box of stone a
box of slots of light an
excrescence of human-animal endeavour a
weather-raped dying shelter a
defenceless hollow crag

yellow signs warn & command
do not enter a histories' crumb
ling fabrication(s) we

> squeeze through prized

apart wire & find some
selves of us with
in a solid Escher-esque closet

algae-splodged & mossily-written-on
block walls drip as hail falls
from sky's printer all
that is 3d-touchable being

                                                built
                                                up in
                                                layers
                                                of un
                                                saids

despite some authority's
black-on-yellow wasp-sharp signs

                                                we find 9

white construction-site hardhats nuzzled
together like albino lady
birds on an

                                                altar
                                                &

aluminium ladders at
jaunty angles giving
access

to greazy battlements where count
less footfalls freeze-froze noise

some i of a Me climbs
up a snake-sm
ooth yet snake-int

ricate calendar on wet aluminium rungs some

shape paces
battlements as a distant
Eigg's jagged anvil flattens & anneals

sea to blade

tide's deep ditch-green fragrance gleams
on castle walls as a loch's pewter ripples
hail-hazed hills pebbles pines bladderwrack & oaks
miniaturise to a memory's brooch

all while white helmets huddle
bodiless: some council in
session as

a buried gauzy energy of their bones cools to begin

fade

Casteal Tioram (pronounced 'chee-rum') is Gaelic for 'dry castle'.

Lightning Source UK Ltd.
Milton Keynes UK
UKOW040640150113

204882UK00001B/8/P